The Poetic "I"

The Poetic "I"

Alternate Voices

KEN BAZYN

RESOURCE *Publications* · Eugene, Oregon

THE POETIC "I"
Alternate Voices

Resource Publications
An Imprint of Wipf and Stock Publishers
199 W. 8th Ave., Suite 3
Eugene, OR 97401

www.wipfandstock.com

PAPERBACK ISBN: 978-1-6667-3222-1
HARDCOVER ISBN: 978-1-6667-2565-0
EBOOK ISBN: 978-1-6667-2566-7

NOVEMBER 22, 2021 11:08 AM

CONTENTS

Acknowledgments

I REJOICE AT THE MARVELOUS HELP I've been given on this new title by my wife, Barbara, who evaluated each line's meaning and significance, offering useful counterproposals, as well the indefatigable David Reynolds, who once again critically examined the final draft, then oversaw the proposed page layout.

What a godsend for religious poets that Wipf & Stock continues to build on and expand their impressive list. My gratitude goes out to Jonathan Hill for well-honed typesetting expertise. I commend Robert Meier for his darkroom skills in developing my 35 mm negatives and Rockbrook Camera in Omaha for painstakingly putting them onto such a fine CD.

These three poems appeared in the following magazines. Thanks!

"The Annual New Year's Party" in *C.S.P. World News*

"The Christmas Tree" in *Parnassus*

"In Old Age" in *Colonnades*

INTRODUCTION

The Multiple Personae Of Fernando Pessoa

"Yo no soy yo.
Soy este ..."
"I am not I.
I am he ... "[1]

—JUAN RAMÓN JIMÉNEZ

ONE SHOULD NEVER ASSUME that the narrator in a poem is expressing views identical to the author's. "For words, like Nature, half reveal / And half conceal the Soul within,"[2] Tennyson wrote in his poem "In Memoriam A.H.H." Autobiographical elements tend to be so mixed in with the fictional that lines blur. The author's memory may be inaccurate or he may prefer to camouflage his true feelings about a private trouble. Or, not wanting to admit to past failures in public, he dilutes the significance of previous incidents. "It is not what is criminal that is hardest to acknowledge," Rousseau declared in *Confessions*, "but what is ridiculous or shameful."[3] The author may have done an about-face (as Goethe did regarding *The Sorrows of Young Werther*) and now is anxious to disown earlier writings. Or he may want to appear less (or more) strident on a controversial subject than he actually is.

Since the poet depends on sound—relying on assonance, alliteration, rhyme, accent and beat—sometimes he may only approximate reality due

1. Hays, *"Eternidades," Selected Writings of Juan Ramón Jiménez*, 86–87.
2. Tennyson, *Poetic and Dramatic Works*, 219.
3. Guterman, *Anchor Book of French Quotations*, 196–97.

to the music he hears. Alternately, he may be eager to enter into the minds of others, filling up his pages with characters of varied temperaments, as well as of a different race, nationality, ethnic group, or gender. For all these reasons and more, modern critics distinguish between four voices: the real-life author, the implied author, the narrator, and the dramatized characters.[4] "The 'I,' perhaps, is no more than a conventional symbol," ventured the French poet and essayist Paul Valéry, "as empty as the verb to be."[5] "A poem, even when it begins with an actual experience," suggests Richard Ellman in his famous study of W.B. Yeats and his masks, "distorts, heightens, simplifies, and transmutes, so that we can say only with many qualifications that a given experience inspired a particular verse."[6] Thus to unravel how one particular poem reflects an author's life or attitudes is no easy matter.

"When I state myself, as the Representative of the Verse," Emily Dickinson wrote to her preceptor, Thomas Wentworth Higginson, "it does not mean—me—but a supposed person."[7] Keats, in a letter to Richard Woodhouse, considered the poet changeable as a chameleon: "the most unpoetical of any thing in existence; because he has no Identity—he is continually in for—and filling some other Body."[8] Breton poet Tristan Corbière refers to his self in "Epitaph" as *mélange adultère de tout*,[9] while Symbolist Jules Laforgue, appearing as the "Lord Chancellor of Analysis" in "Sundays," found such a motley crew within himself that it was necessary to let each one have its say,[10] for the "I" is but "a poor, pale and paltry individual who believes in his Self only in absent-minded moments."[11] Baudelaire, in "Crowds," acknowledged: "The poet enjoys the incomparable privilege of being able to be himself or someone else, just as he chooses. Like those wandering souls who go about looking for a body, he enters as he likes into each man's personality."[12]

4. Gudas, "Persona," 901.

5. Valéry, *Collected Works, Volume 2*, 313.

6. Ellmann, *Yeats: Man and His Masks*, 5.

7. Dickinson, "July, 1862," 306.

8. Keats, "To Richard Woodhouse," 113.

9. Rees, *French Poetry: 1820–1950*, 265. ("adulterous mixture of all things")

10. Hamburger, *Truth of Poetry*, 54–55.

11. Rees, *French Poetry: 1820–1950*, 351.

12. Baudelaire, *Paris Spleen: 1869*, 20.

When a person writes a letter, he inevitably shows a different side of himself to each recipient, depending on their exact relationship, the purpose and occasion of his writing.[13] "Writing," Quaker novelist Jessamyn West proclaims, becomes "a way of playing parts, of trying on masks, of assuming roles."[14] "It is the feelings of the empirical self which poetry enlarges, complements, or even replaces with fictitious ones," critic Michael Hamburger argues, for "the empirical self is not the whole self, cramped as it is in its shell of convention, habit, and circumstance."[15] Indeed, several centuries before, Montaigne had enjoined, "The fairest souls are those that have the most variety and adaptability."[16] Simply by learning a foreign language, T.S. Eliot believed, we acquire "a kind of supplemental personality."[17]

The true artist, according to modern Portuguese poet Fernando Pessoa (in an article entitled "Ultimatum" under the heteronym of Alvaro de Campos), should be capable of feeling for others—past, present, and future—who are *unlike* himself.[18] "If each man were not able to live a number of other lives besides his own," wrote French poet and essayist Paul Valéry, "he would not be able to live his own life."[19] "Every person who consists of several persons," insists German poet Novalis in one of his "Miscellaneous Fragments," "is a person raised to a higher power."[20] It comes as no surprise then that behavioral psychologists will emphasize the importance of role-playing in personality growth.[21]

Yes, "the poet's good at pretending," Pessoa comments in "Self-Analysis."[22] For a start, he is able to create fictional characters. Recall Robert Browning's adept use of dramatic monologues, bringing to life a medieval rabbi, a twelfth-century troubadour, a Roman Catholic bishop, a Reformation Antinomian, an Arab physician, an impoverished nobleman, an eighteenth-century German musician, a first-century Greek poet, and a

13. Booth, *Rhetoric of Fiction*, 71.
14. West, "The Slave Cast Out," 202.
15. Hamburger, *Truth of Poetry*, 147.
16. Montaigne, *Complete Essays of Montaigne*, 621.
17. Eliot, *On Poetry and Poets*, 8.
18. Pessoa, *Selected Poems*, 20. Cf. Pessoa, *Selected Prose*, 83.
19. Valéry, *Art of Poetry*, 58.
20. Novalis, *Hymns to the Night*, 70.
21. Gudas, "Persona," 901.
22. Pessoa, *Selected Poems*, 75.

Florentine painter, among others.[23] In Rimbaud's hallucinatory "Night in Hell," the narrator ejaculates, "I am a master of phantasmagoria,"[24]while in Louis Aragon's "Richard II Forty," the narrator rhythmically repeats, "I remain king of my griefs."[25] Such postures permit the poet to take up different viewpoints, without making an overarching commitment. "Of the many men whom I am, whom we are," announced the bewildered Chilean poet Pablo Neruda in "We Are Many," "I cannot settle on a single one."[26] Baudelaire tied his "love of disguise and of masks" together with his "passion for journeying:"[27] "Music," he exclaimed, "takes me like a sea! Towards my pale star, beneath a misty ceiling or in a vast ether I set sail."[28] In a letter to the editor of *Presença*, Pessoa elaborated, "I do not evolve, I simply JOURNEY . . . I continuously change personality."[29]

There is a real fluidity in many a poet's identity. In "Brotherhood," the disillusioned twentieth-century French poet André Frénaud complained that even while sorting through familiar memories, he could no longer recognize the child that he had once been.[30] Von Hofmannsthal took up, in turn, the voice of a ship's cook, the emperor of China, an old man eager for summer, as well as both a grandmother and a grandson,[31] while that most versatile of modern poetic actors, Ezra Pound, made translations or paraphrases from Chinese, Anglo-Saxon, French, Italian, Egyptian, Hindi, Japanese, Latin, and Provençal.[32] "Thus I am Dante for a space and am / One Francois Villon," he asserted in "Histrion."[33] "I began this search for the real in a book called *Personae*," Pound confesses, "casting off, as it were, complete masks of the self in each poem. I continued in a long series of translations, which were but more elaborate masks."[34] Here the poet

23. Browning, *Poems of Robert Browning*, 477–541.

24. Bernard, *Rimbaud*, 315.

25. Woledge, et al., *Penguin Book of French Verse*, 617–19.

26. Reid, "We Are Many," 528.

27. Hamburger, *Truth in Poetry*, 53.

28. Rees, *French Poetry 1820–1950*, 151.

29. Pessoa, *Selected Prose*, 263.

30. Woledge, et al., *Penguin Book of French Verse*, 637.

31. Stork, *Lyrical Poems of Hugo Von Hofmannsthal*, 45–54.

32. Pound, *Ezra Pound: Translations*, 7–8.

33. Pound, *New Selected Poems and Translations*, 8.

34. Pound, *A Memoir of Gaudier-Brzeska*, 85.

appears like some master ventriloquist pulling the strings of marionettes,[35] with *Cathay* usually considered his greatest triumph.[36] How sharply this contrasts with the Romantic notion of a poet who feels intensely, then expresses himself directly in exclamations, statements, and questions through strong imagery—all of which can be verified by the poet's letters and journals. Keats referred to this stance as the "egotistical sublime,"[37] while Jules Laforgue called it, *Moi-le-Magnifique* ("I-the-Magnificent"),[38] since the poet's voice is loud and sharp.

At times a poet's identity may be temporarily lost in a kaleidoscope of distorted reflections. "The magic mirror where I always looked the same has shattered," mourns Pessoa in "In Lisbon Revisited (1926)," under the heteronym Alvaro de Campos. "And in each fateful fragment I see only a piece of me."[39] "What must I do to single out myself? / How can I put myself together?"[40] wondered Pablo Neruda. Twentieth-century poet and critic Yves Bonnefoy sought to investigate "the threads that unite things *within* me,"[41] while Pound, near the end of his magnificent *Cantos* seemed to throw up his hands, "I cannot make it cohere."[42] Catholic playwright Paul Claudel, speaking of Gide, appeared to label the entire enterprise of journal-writing as "a series of poses" by someone who is fascinated by mirrors, in short, "a monument of insincerity."[43]

One ponders: is sincerity the cardinal literary virtue as Rousseau espoused? "We wear the mask that grins and lies," acknowledged nineteenth-century African-American poet Paul Laurence Dunbar, "It hides our cheeks and shades our eyes."[44] "Each of us does his best to hide behind a shield," Christian psychologist Paul Tournier decided after years of consultations. "For one it is mysterious silence which constitutes an impenetrable retreat. For another it is the facile chit chat, so that we never seem to get near him. Or else it is the erudition, quotations, abstractions,

---

35. Hamburger, *Truth in Poetry*, 123.

36. Pritchard, *Lives of the Modern Poets*, 154–55.

37. Abrams, *Mirror and the Lamp*, 95–99. Cf. Keats, "To Richard Woodhouse," 113.

38. Laforgue, "A Paul Bourget," 3–4. Cf. Hamburger, *Truth in Poetry*, 51.

39. Pessoa, *A Little Larger Than the Entire Universe*, 220.

40. Reid, "We Are Many," 528.

41. Hamburger, *Truth in Poetry*, 241.

42. Pound, "Canto CXVI," *Cantos*, 796.

43. Russell, *Correspondence between Paul Claudel and André Gide*, 235.

44. Mandelbaum and Richardson, "We Wear the Mask," 484.

theories, academic argument, technical jargon; or ready-made answers, trivialities, or sententious and patronizing advice. One hides behinds his timidity, so that we cannot find anything to say to him; another behind a fine self-assurance."[45] Only a man's spirit knows his deepest thoughts, avows St. Paul (1 Cor. 2:11)—or, one might add, those to whom he chooses to reveal himself. "Is it not true that one man never completely understands another?" asks Kierkegaard in *Works of Love*.[46] In *Parallel Lives*, the ancient Greek biographer Plutarch likened the unknown portions of his subjects' souls to old maps beyond which are "prodigies and fables" where "nothing is certain or credible."[47] Even James Boswell, perhaps the greatest biographer in English, after having conversed with Samuel Johnson countless times, read through his prayers and meditations, and recovered hundreds of private letters, could never determine why Johnson counted his steps or touched lampposts.[48]

Some believe that we can, and should, write only about what we have experienced. "The most persuasive poets," concluded Aristotle in *The Poetics*, chapter 17, "are those who have the same natures as their characters and enter into their sufferings; he who feels distress represents distress and he who feels anger represents anger most genuinely."[49] This is a sentiment echoed later in Horace's *Art of Poetry*: "if you would have me weep, you must first of all feel grief yourself."[50] Cicero required the orator to be burning first if he wished to inflame others: *Ardeat, qui vult incendere*. This precept was echoed and expanded upon by Quintilian, *Prius afficiamur ipsi, ut alios afficiamus*.[51] But to claim that you must live through an experience before commenting on it is going too far. Otherwise, only former drug addicts could ever declaim against heroin, adulterers against unfaithfulness, traitors on treason. Moralists could peal out their warnings only after they had fallen into the vices they so rightly abhor.

45. Tournier, *Meaning of Persons*, 143.

46. Kierkegaard, *Works of Love*, 216.

47. Plutarch, *Rise and Fall of Athens*, 13.

48. Lewis, "The Difficult Art of Biography," 65.

49. Gilbert, *Literary Criticism*, 94.

50. Gilbert, *Literary Criticism*, 131.

51. Jones, *A New Dictionary of Quotations*, 430. ("Let him, who wishes to rouse and inflame the feelings of others, show that he himself is impassioned." "Let us first show by our manner that we ourselves are *really* affected by what we say, so that we may affect or influence others, may work on the feelings of others.") Cf. Cole and Chinoy, *Actors on Acting*, 22.

Or is spontaneity the one reliable ink blot test: is the first thing which enters into your head the most likely to be true? The French novelist Stendhal (among others) argued that to write well, one must write fast, transcribing one's impressions, or the subconscious promptings of one's interior monologue, without organization or reflection.[52] "I'm making it a rule not to stand on ceremony and never to erase,"[53]he declared at the beginning of his private diaries. Rousseau came to dread a consistent, overarching style, which he believed artificial and monotonous. "I shall not waste time in making the style uniform; I shall always have whichever style comes to me, I shall change it according to my moods, I shall say each thing as I feel it, as I see it."[54] Or think of the automatic writing so prominent among the Surrealists. Twentieth-century French poet Robert Desnos had a remarkable ability to go into a kind of "hypnotic sleep," where he cultivated strange, dream-like symbols and haunting incantations.[55] Freud was to urge his followers to tap into the unconscious through free association. Read through Corbière's *Sleep Litany* with its haphazard jumble of incongruous images.[56] To achieve a more authentic stream of consciousness, Surrealist poet Guillaume Apollinaire even did away with punctuation,[57] while Proust, in his novels, forged the meandering sentence (*phrase à tiroirs*), in which one clause is jammed into another.[58] "Did unknown words sing upon your lips," inquired Symbolist poet Stéphane Mallarmé, "accursed shreds of an absurd sentence?"[59]

While speed may be fine for a diary or a journal, when it comes to memoir or autobiography, it's best to step back, slowly reworking one's initial impressions into ever more exquisite and polished prose. Aesthetically, do you prefer a passage in Thoreau's journals or his later re-working, *Walden, or Life in the Woods*? First he recorded entries in his journal, ("field notes" he once called them), "winnowed" these into lectures, which were later turned into essays to eventually become part of a book.[60] "Disconnected

52. Peyre, *Literature and Sincerity*, 7.
53. Sage, "April 18, 1801," 6.
54. Peyre, *Literature and Sincerity*, 87–88.
55. Rees, *French Poetry: 1820–1950*, 744.
56. Rees, *French Poetry: 1820–1950*, 244, 251–63.
57. Rees, *French Poetry: 1820–1950*, 538.
58. Barzun, *From Dawn to Decadence*, 716.
59. Rees, *French Poetry: 1820–1950*, 213.
60. Young, *Spiritual Journal of Henry David Thoreau*, 58–59.

thoughts" were written down, brought into "juxtaposition" with earlier ideas, until whole new fields of endeavor would come into view.[61] And, for that matter, why should a diary entry be more honest and straightforward than a maxim forged out of life's vicissitudes?

Look at early drafts by famous poets compared to their later reformulations. In *Visions and Revisions*, Barry Wallenstein cites a number of such instances. The opening stanza of Wilfred Owen's "Anthem for Dead Youth" once began:

> "What passing bells for those who die so fast?
> —Only the monstrous anger of our guns.
> Let the majestic insults of their iron mouths
> Be as the requiem of burials."

The final version of these same lines reads:

> "What passing-bells for those who die as cattle?
> Only the monstrous anger of the guns,
> Only the stuttering rifles' rapid rattle
> Can patter out their hasty orisons."[62]

Notice the difference?

Let me now more closely examine that great modern exemplar of multiple personalities, Portuguese poet Fernando Pessoa (1888–1935). He wrote under perhaps seventy-five different names, taking on the character of a bookkeeper, a philosopher, an astrologer, assorted translators and diarists, a girl dying of tuberculosis, and a nobleman who commits suicide.[63] When he was a child his family moved to South Africa, where he grew up in an English-speaking school in Durban. He returned in 1905 to Portugal, where he wrote most of his mature work in Portuguese. As an adolescent, he had invented a series of newspapers with news, commentary, and jokes by a fictional team of journalists. His first poems, written in English, were attributed to Charles Robert Anon, later to Alexander Search. Then, in a sudden burst of creativity in 1914, he conjured up four major poetic selves, or heteronyms, each with his own distinctive style:[64] Alvaro de Campos was a naval engineer fascinated by Walt Whitman; Alberto Caeiro was a

---

61. Paul, *Shores of America*, 295.

62. Wallenstein, *Vision and Revisions*, 88–89.

63. Pessoa, *The Book of Disquiet*, 505–509.

64. Pessoa, *Selected Prose*, 255–59.

bucolic poet trumpeting the simple life; Ricardo Reis was a melancholy doctor much enamored with Horace's odes; while "Fernando Pessoa" was an all-round experimentalist. This methodology clearly revealed Pessoa's loathing for simplistic answers and reductionist philosophies. "In every corner of my soul," he declared, under the heteronym of Alvaro de Campos, "stands an altar to a different god."[65] Or perhaps he hoped to see all sides of a question simultaneously like a Cubist artist whose aim was to depict not only the front view of an object, but each successive face as well, as though walking all around it.[66]

Nineteenth-century existentialist Danish philosopher Soren Kierkegaard had already issued works under a series of pseudonyms, each meant to convey a coherent perspective on a particular subject: Victor Eremita (editor of *Either/Or*), Johannes de Silentio (author of *Fear and Trembling*), Constantine Constantius (author of the first half of *Repetition*), Hilarius Bookbinder (editor of *Stages on Life's Way*), Johannes Climacus (author of *Concluding Unscientific Postscript*), and Anti-Climacus (author of *Practice in Christianity*). "The individual has manifold shadows, all of which resemble him and from time to time have an equal claim to be the man himself," Kierkegaard pointed out in *The Repetition*. Biographer William Lowry imagined Kierkegaard to be playing a game of hide-and-seek, in which he fully expected to be found,[67] while biographer Joakim Garff believed these pseudonyms allowed Kierkegaard to write about ideas which were so private he couldn't even put them into his journals.[68]

Pessoa wanted to be true to each of his heteronyms, inhabiting their education, temperament, and philosophy of life. Occasionally they even argue with each other. "For some psychological reason . . . I constructed within myself several characters who are distinct from each other and from me," Pessoa observed, "and to whom I attributed several poems which are not such as I, with my own feelings and ideas, would write . . . Many of them express ideas I do not accept, and feelings I have never felt."[69] One of his earliest memories was how, at the age of six, he had written letters to himself signed by a French knight, Chevalier de Pas. "Ever since I was a child," he told Adolfo Casais Monteiro, "it has been my tendency to create around me

65. Pessoa, *Selected Poems*, 49.
66. Barzun, *From Dawn to Decadence*, 647.
67. Lowrie, *Kierkegaard, Volume 1*, 287–89.
68. Garff, *Soren Kierkegaard*, 362–63.
69. Pessoa, *Selected Poems*, 23.

a fictitious world, to surround myself with friends and acquaintances that never existed."[70]

In another letter to Monteiro, he asserts, "What I am essentially—behind the involuntary masks of poet, logical reasoner and so forth—is a dramatist."[71] Elsewhere, he sees his poems as "dramas" divided, not into theatrical acts, but separate characters.[72] In a similar way, French novelist André Gide wrote in his journal on November 15, 1923: "Certainly it is easier for me to put words into a character's mouth than to express myself in my own name—and particularly when the character I am creating differs most from me . . . I become the other person."[73] Soon, however, Pessoa found the persona of Alberto Caeiro so untenable that he attributed only a few poems to him after 1920. Ricardo Reis echoes Latin phrases which Pessoa mocks; he "writes better than I, but with a purism I find excessive."[74] Indeed, if one were to read Pessoa's poems exactly in chronological order, one would be shocked by the disharmonies and contradictions expressed within the space of just a few days.[75]

Surely one of the great monuments of Western prose is the dialogues of Plato. Pre-Socratic philosophers tended to write in aphorisms or riddles—almost as though they were uttering oracles from the gods. Plato's earliest descriptions of Socrates, however, resemble dramatic vignettes. The unexamined life isn't worth living, said his hero, who in the marketplace would pose such momentous questions as "What is justice?" "What is piety?" "What is temperance?" When a person responded, Socrates raised follow-up questions to demonstrate how shallow and flawed the original reply had been. However, the ongoing discussion/interrogation rarely led to a mutually satisfactory conclusion. Indeed, later skeptics took Socrates' method further, declaring that a comprehensive answer wasn't even possible.[76] Still, Aristotle in *Metaphysics* insists there is real merit in any person who expresses even "superficial views; for these also contributed something,"[77] perhaps by putting a subject in sharper focus or exposing an

70. Pessoa, *Selected Prose*, 254.

71. Pessoa, *Selected Prose*, 263.

72. Pessoa, *Selected Prose*, 262.

73. Gide, *The Counterfeiters* with *Journal of "The Counterfeiters,"* 439.

74. Pessoa, *Selected Prose*, 259.

75. Pessoa, *Selected Poems*, 38–39.

76. Cary, *Philosophy and Religion in the West*, Parts 1–3, 5–8.

77. Ross, "Metaphysics," 1570.

obviously flawed viewpoint. "I am a creature of dialogue," cried novelist André Gide, "everything in me is conflicting and contradictory."[78] "I no longer really know who I am; or, if you prefer: I never *am*; I am *becoming*."[79] His groping via fictional characters was a way of clarifying his own thinking.[80] "If I am sincere with myself (but I fear one lies more to one's self than to any one else)," Lord Byron confided in his diary on December 6, 1813, "every page should confute, refute, and utterly abjure its predecessor."[81]

Sociologists speak of the "Rashomon effect," based on a movie by Japanese director Akira Kurosawa, where each character, in turn, seeks to understand the key event in the plot: possibly a rape and a murder. We hear from the samurai's wife, the bandit who held up the couple, a woodcutter who was in the vicinity, even the dead samurai himself—speaking through a medium. Did the bandit kill the samurai in a sword fight? Had he been urged on by the wife? Or perhaps the wife herself stabbed the victim in a troubled state of mind? Or did the samurai actually commit hara-kiri? The audience is left to work out its own solution from the perplexing threads of evidence.[82] Kurosawa's plot itself was stitched together from two short stories by Ryunosuke Akutagawa: "In a Grove" and "Rashomon."[83]

In modern courts of law, the prosecution and the defense bring in witnesses who offer at times conflicting testimony; cross-examination by the lawyers helps to elucidate who is telling the truth. The jurors must reconstruct what really happened to decide on the defendant's guilt. Or what of the early church's ultimate acceptance of four canonical gospels (Matthew, Mark, Luke, and John), each having its own peculiar slant? Believers apparently felt this was the best way to fully encompass the extraordinary life of Christ. The Gospels, despite varying details, nuances, and chronologies, do agree on the central truth of his deity and resurrection. An airbrushed, closely-edited harmony just wouldn't do justice to a figure who had so profoundly broken the mold of what it was to be human. Modern American novelist Marilynne Robinson recently published a tetralogy on the fictional town of Gilead, Iowa, each written from a different character's vantage point: *Gilead* by pastor John Ames; *Home* by his best friend, Robert Boughton; *Lila*, by

---

78. Gide, *If It Die*, 234.
79. Gide, "February 8, 1927," *The Journals: 1914–1927*, 393.
80. Peyre, *Literature and Sincerity*, 293.
81. Byron, *Byron, A Self-Portrait*, 234.
82. Kracauer, *Theory of Film*, 277–79.
83. Akutagawa, *Rashomon and Other Stories*, 15–39.

Ames' wife; and *Jack*, by Boughton's wayward son. Readers are left to decide which account is most convincing.

And what of the multitude in Shakespeare's head? From the same mind leaps Prospero, Falstaff, Macbeth, and Lear. Shakespeare is a virtuoso at disguises. Iago's "I am not what I am,"[84] remarks critic Lionel Trilling, can also stand for Rosalind not being a boy, Portia not a doctor of the law, Duke Vincentio not a friar, Hamlet not a madman, Edgar not Tom o' Bedlam, etc.[85] "You can tell anything," novelist Marcel Proust once advised Gide concerning his memoirs, "but on condition that you never say: *I*."[86] This is not unlike the comments of legendary Scribners' editor Maxwell Perkins to F. Scott Fitzgerald concerning a character in *The Beautiful and the Damned*; "Now, you are, through Maury, expressing your views, of course; but you would do so differently if you were deliberately stating them as your views."[87] In the Gospels, Jesus warns of hypocrites who are wolves in "sheep's clothing" (Matt. 7:15) or "whitewashed tombs" (Matt. 23:27). Such figures are rampant in Western literature. Think of Moliere's Tartuffe, Fielding's Captain Blifil, Balzac's Cousin Bette, Dickens' Uriah Heep, Hawthorne's Roger Chillingworth, Thackeray's Becky Sharp, and so on.[88] Hypocrisy is a trap one can fall into. "I put on someone else's fancy dress," Pessoa avers under the heteronym Alvaro de Campos, but people saw through me. "When I tried to take off the mask, / It was stuck to my face."[89]

What, too, of the age-old paradox of the actor? Should he actually feel the emotion he projects or merely become more adept at displaying it? "The actor is not, and cannot be, sincere, that is to say, he cannot experience a true emotion and take himself, even temporarily, for the character whose part he is playing," says literary critic Henri Peyre, describing the views of Enlightenment thinker Denis Diderot. "His task is to produce an illusion, but not to produce it in himself. If he must cry, let it be 'like the seducer at the feet of a woman whom he does not love, but whom he wants to deceive.'"[90] Diderot had been impressed by the famous actor David Garrick's ability to

84. Craig, "*Othello, Act I, Scene 1*," 796.

85. Trilling, *Sincerity and Authenticity*, 13–14.

86. Gide, *Journals of André Gide, Volume I*, 304.

87. Wheelock, "December 12, 1921," 31.

88. Trilling, *Sincerity and Authenticity*, 15.

89. Pessoa, *Selected Poems*, 105.

90. Peyre, *Literature and Sincerity*, 75.

entertain his friends with all manner of facial expressions and emotions, while having no genuine feelings himself.[91] Aren't poets rather like actors? What is the reader to make of Emily Dickinson's religious beliefs? At times she appears a sincere Christian, a nature mystic, or an agnostic. In the end, which is she? She probably felt sympathy for each position and refused to be pinned down.

Such a capacity allows the poet to examine more fully the "what ifs" and paradoxes of life. "Just what makes me suppose / That there is beauty in things," Pessoa inquires under the heteronym Alberto Caeiro,[92] while, under the heteronym of Alvaro de Campos, he speculates, "If at some point in time / I had turned left instead of right, . . . said yes instead of no;"[93] "here I am the conundrum / That keeps them all guessing at provincial parties."[94] Under the heteronym of Ricardo Reis, he proclaims, "I feel / That who I am and who I was / Are different dreams."[95] Under the heteronym of Alvaro de Campos, he wonders aloud about a particularly moving passage, "Where did this come from? It's too good to be mine."[96]

How does all this relate to Christianity? Acts of the Apostles (11:26) claims the early disciples were first called "Christians" in Antioch; this term probably means followers, or associates, of Christ.[97] Years after his conversion to Anglo-Catholicism, T.S. Eliot has Lord Clareton's ghost in "The Elder Statesman" announce, "I've been freed from the self that pretends to be someone / And in becoming no one, I begin to live."[98] In Eliot's criticism, he urged the poet to do away with personality.[99] But does the Christian actually destroy the old self, or perhaps deepen the authentic one? The apostle Paul characterizes the Christian way of life: "I have been crucified with Christ; and it is no longer I who live, but it is Christ who lives in me" (Gal. 2:19–20). This paradox is taken up by German metaphysical poet Paul Fleming in "Devotion:" "I live; yet 'tis not I. He lives in me, /

91. Diderot, *The Paradox of Acting*, 20, 32–33.

92. Pessoa, *Selected Poems*, 127.

93. Pessoa, *Selected Poems*, 109.

94. Pessoa, *Selected Poems*, 115.

95. Pessoa, *Selected Poems*, 159.

96. Pessoa, *Selected Poems*, 121.

97. Mounce, *Mounce's Complete Expository Dictionary*, 110.

98. Eliot, *The Elder Statesman*, 129.

99. Eliot, "Tradition and the Individual Talent," *Selected Prose*, 26. "The progress of an artist is a continual self-sacrifice, a continual extinction of personality."

. . . My life to him was death, his death my life."[100] Assuming the stance of a friar, in "Stations of the Cross," Pessoa writes, "Sent as the envoy of an unknown king, / I carry out vague promptings from beyond, / . . . I feel that I am no one but the shadow / Of a shape that awes me though I see it not."[101] How much the true self is submerged and how much it is fully on display in Christianity is rather difficult to decide.

Like Goethe's Faust, each of us must admit that "two souls abide, alas, within my breast."[102] An internal divided self appeared in Western literature as early as Homer's *Iliad*, where one encounters interior monologues with the recurring phrase *alla ti e moi tauta philos dielexato thymos*[103] ("then why does the heart within me debate these things?").[104] In 1880 French poet Paul Verlaine explained, concerning his conversion, "My work was cut into two very distinct portions . . . volumes in which Catholicism displays its logic and its illecebrancies, its blandishments and its terrors, and others of a purely worldly and sensual character. I believe and I am a good Christian one moment; the next minute I believe and I am a bad Christian."[105] How similar this is to the profound dilemma Paul expressed in Romans chapter 7, lacerated as he was by diametrically-opposed pulls from the flesh and the spirit.

The French Romantic author Chateaubriand, known for his apologetic work, *Genius of Christianity*, confesses, "Before my death, I want above all . . . to explain my unexplainable heart."[106] If one wants eternal fame, counseled Edgar Allen Poe, that master of Gothic terrors, one should write a little book entitled "My Heart Laid Bare." He goes on, "but to write it, *there* is the rub . . . No man *could* write it, even if he dared. The paper would shrivel and blaze at every touch of the fiery pen."[107] Imagine your hidden prejudices, fears, lusts, and hates revealed on some overhead projector. You would be too embarrassed to appear in public! That's a real

100. Warnke, *European Metaphysical Poetry*, 182–83.

101. Pessoa, *Selected Poems*, 66–69.

102. Goethe, *Faust*, 42.

103. Scholes and Kellogg, *The Nature of Narrative*, 179.

104. Lattimore, *The Iliad of Homer*, 245, 356, 433, 438. Odysseus (XI, line 407), Menelaus (XVII, line 97), Agenor (XXI, line 562), Hector (XXII, line 122).

105. Peyre, *Literature and Sincerity*, 158–59. "Illecebrancies" was a Latinism coined by Verlaine from *illecebra* or "seductive charm."

106. Halsall, "*Memoires D'Outre-Tombe*," 725.

107. Stern, "The Impossibility of Writing a Truthful Autobiography," 651.

problem, contends Albert Thibaudet, since the autobiographer dredges up only what he has consciously retrieved from memory, crafting his life into an "artificial unity," while the novelist's extraordinary range of characters allows for "profound multiplicity."[108] "The being of beasts is a one way track," trumpeted Surrealist Pierre Reverdy, "that of man is a dual or a multiple highway; it always stands at a crossroad."[109]

Human beings oscillate, are illogical, inconsistent. In the end, masks, multiple personalities, and ambiguity are at the heart of a genuine poet. Critic Sigurd Burckhardt contends, "A word which can function simultaneously as two or more different parts of speech, a phrase that can be parsed in two or more ways—to the despair of all teachers of grammar—simply extends the pervasive incertitude of poetry from words to their connections into statements."[110] Ambiguity, notes William Empson in his landmark work, *Seven Types of Ambiguity*, may be deliberate, due to indecision, or reflect confusion of thought.[111] There lies "complexity, associative and connotative richness, texture, and the possibility of irony," according to Burkhardt, for "the poet as a fool must be a corrupter of words, a punster, rhymester, verbal trickster, for there is no other way to break the disgraceful bonds into which words have fallen."[112]

"You want people to always be consistent," guffawed Rousseau. "I doubt that is possible for man."[113] "In every poetical production," Diderot noticed, "there is always a little lying, the limits of which is not, and will never be, determined."[114] Why not then embrace and celebrate your contradictions and come to terms with them? Which of Rembrandt's multiple self-portraits is the true one? Which of the Karamazov brothers most resembles Dostoyevsky? Is Soren Kierkegaard more like John Climacus or Anti-Climacus? Is the genuine Pessoa closest to himself or one of his heteronyms? And which poetic "I" best expresses the authentic you? The poses are ways of probing. "Writing is a fire that lifts up a great confusion of ideas," affirms free-wheeling modernist French poet Blaise Cendrars, "and incinerates groups of images before reducing them to crackling embers and

---

108. Peyre, *Literature and Sincerity*, 210.
109. Peyre, *Literature and Sincerity*, 321.
110. Burckhardt, *Shakespearean Meanings*, 31.
111. Empson, *Seven Types of Ambiguity*, 5–6.
112. Burckhardt, *Shakespearean Meanings*, 32, 45.
113. Rousseau, *Julie, or The New Heloise*, 20.
114. Peyre, *Literature and Sincerity*, 326.

falling ashes. But the spontaneity of the fire remains mysterious. To write is to burn alive, but is also to be reborn from ashes."[115]

---

115. Reese, *French Poetry 1820–1950*, 571–72.

Incurvatus in se

"A self-made man is as likely as a self-laid egg."
—ATTRIBUTED TO MARK TWAIN

Me, Me, and don't forget I,
a baby's hymn, a lover's sigh,
a concrete ubiquitous pronoun
definitely vainglorious.

Who is it the sounding trumpets hail,
who brays the loudest,
gawks in every looking-glass
and pats his own shoulder blade?

A microcosm of plenitude,
self-fulfiller of prophecies,
paragon of Christian *and* pagan virtues—
homo arrogantus.

Ego this and ego that,
narcissistic potentate,
a rabble-rousing son of Cain,
Charity's my nom de plume,
enfant terrible's my fame.

Unadulterated pride
announces its arrival,
puffs itself up for a raise,
preserves its own damned independence.

What of my genius?
    my legacy?
    my memoirs?
    my infallibility?

Whose bootstraps completed the task?
who set the table and then helped himself?
whose cunning cornered Fortuna?
whom should every fool lie prostrate before?

God himself stands in awe,
the angels raise the rafters,
the cherubim and seraphim
glorify my credentials.

But it seems I
must always stand in relation to others,
humiliating! that the standard
must be measured against obvious imperfection.

i

i
a period
on a pedestal.

I
a slender hope
with a roof and a foundation.

A Slumbering Cradle

Who's rocking my slumbering cradle
with soft, yet penetrating sighs?
I shiver even while wrapped up
in hand-knit quilts and flannel pajamas,
I doze uncertain,
for the rocker's hand is tenuous, self-absorbed,
when I cry
milk flows robust from supersaturate nipples,
still, I detect a definite holding back.

I wobble my head
and stare in incomprehension
since this room appears an inverted bowl,
why does everyone turn their head toward this newborn howler?
I splash about my tub,
while mom patty-cakes my rear end,
it's so exhilarating to be lifted high,
bang my head against some revolving mobile,
be tossed about like a smiling ball,
rub noses with Eskimo relatives.

Uncle makes corkscrew faces,
Sis, frog croakings with her tongue,
my brain is in my mouth,
for how can one understand what
hasn't been bitten or sucked on?
I look silly as an overturned beetle
who can't quite right himself,

show me a mirror: who dat?
I love furry tails,
though I have trouble focusing
on anything not placed directly in my hand.

A cradle is a warm, sheltering oval
but none, I think, do make their fortunes there,
I want something I can pursue and hold on to tight,
for a baby has immense tactile needs,
can be easily dropped and bruised,
and has as much hair as a nectarine.

The Carousel

I throw my foot in the stirrup,
grasp the pommel,
ride a musical horse.
The countryside spins
in an elfin circle
as if under a wizard's spell.
The calliope bangs out
a romantic, not classical, oeuvre,
bulbs twitter, mirrors wobble,
Rapunzel throws down her hair.

Maroon elephants, maize tigers, lime gazelles,
maharajahs, Hungarian princesses
stalk behemoths and imaginary birds.
Mom and dad smile and wave
or hold their voyager tightly in saddle.
Expressionistic caramel apples, corn dogs,
peppermint on an all-day stick—
I'm sucked out of Dorothy's Kansas
by Denslow's art nouveau scarecrow,
tin woodman and cowardly lion.

Up and down through Sinbad adventures,
round and round after outlaws,
gangsters, marauding pirates—
all too quickly my dime disappears
down an attendant's pocket.

Screams of "Again!" "Once more!"
Mom objects: "He's overtired;"
on her shoulder I cuddle up
to a galloping dream.

The Christmas Tree

I remember the bubbling lights and the silver tree,
a game of Parcheesi and marmalade,
Santa's arrival but no jangling sleigh.

I remember a blowing manger and an overturned crib,
Perry Como in staccato with the wrapping paper,
and the year mama knit her brood stocking hats.

I remember so many chocolates my tongue begins to wag,
skiing over the corn stubble,
thawing out my mittens.

I can still see sister's plywood kitchen,
brother's pellet gun/pool table,
and recall our misgivings about our presents.

I remember Hercules sucking Alcmene's teats,
happy children sapping their parents' strength,
sleeping lightly on the 24th.

I remember humming "Holy Night,"
God papering the grass with cattail dust,
being hoisted to the ceiling in grampa's arms.

I remember twinkling paternal faces,
15-year-old dreams puncturing reality,
one generation's blunders transcended for an hour.

I remember Daniel's friends (from Sunday School)
roaring out this world's dime & nickel men,
warming their imagination in a Babylonian flame,

most of all, I remember love.

Glitter, Glitter

Tinkle, tinkle, glitter, glitter,
the sound of the Western Christmas,
talcum powder snow and aluminum trees,
plastic angels and identical tokens of our esteem,
ho-hoing clowns in red-and-white pajamas,
strife-torn nations preaching the Prince of Peace,
yet still the void of desperation,
I can't hear the oxen or the asses bray,
nor lowly shepherds pray,
nor wise men bearing hearts of flesh,
all I know is: tinkle, tinkle, glitter, glitter,
the sound of the Western Christmas.

Adolescence

What harm in crying under the cratered moon?
wolves howl just as freely,
neighborhood dogs orchestrate their yelps.

Wet pillows dry faster than Horus' flight,
da Vinci curves draw us toward their source—
a kite tail flapping against my future.

The young ladies seem so remote, lovers star-mangled,
mares must be fondled, bits taken out,
at fifteen I'm awkward, brash and sorry.

Plucked plumes soon wilt,
desires are fake as the Kensington Rune,
would that Moses or Elijah spoke.

Scared to confide in omni-purple parents,
friends? funny bones or butt-joints,
moods as rootless as air plants.

We're sailing for Prester John's fabulous kingdom
like peg-leg Ahab
on a boat without a rudder.

Coleridge pledges opium visions
as elusive as Buddha's footprints
or Wordsworth's trail of glory.

Like St. George doing battle with the green dragon,
I'll slit the magic knot, or like Plato's demiurge
suture my *Weltseele,* cross from teenybopper to adult.

My Brother

A morning and an evening have passed
since I last saw my brother
hiding behind the peony bush,
grilling anthills with our squirt guns,
knocking each other off the jungle gym,
pushing toy tractors through the sandbox,
playing batter-up with rocks and a sawed-off broom.

Happy they seemed, the days gone by,
but it's hard to remember an average time.
Once in a while home movies help me recall
birthday parties and my first puppy,
our vacation in Florida and Sundays with Aunt Ruby.
But mostly it's myth
that preserves the past—
images warped by gastronomic juices.

Lost in the cornfield when it's 90 degrees,
eating half a hot dog and throwing up after,
digging up nightcrawlers with grampa,
hitting a double with the bases loaded,
attempting to swallow milk already curdled,
watching baby sparrows chirp in their nest,
throwing down a plastic rifle—stitching up my brother's head.

My brother and I did everything together.
The first time he was sick at school
and left early—I cried all recess.
When one of us was spanked,
the other one whimpered.
When I received a new bike,
in four months he could ride beside me.
Until I was twelve, I didn't need a friend.

But there comes a point
in every man's life
when his and his brother's paths
must diverge.
Who knows but they'll
meet at some future crossing,
yet for now part the best of pals,
sorry to see each other go,
knowing how liaisons can stalemate—
say good-bye through
fewer and fewer invitations.

A morning and an evening have passed
since I last saw my brother.
Perhaps he'll come again,
but I don't know when.

i remember . . . Vietnam

i remember
    a rusting fuselage riddled with 55 mm. machine-gun fire,
    two limbless torsos that could fit onto a Samsonite carry-on,
    a calfskin billfold flung open to a grinning six-year-old kid,
    a gleaming West Point casket: drip-dry and ochre.

i remember
    August's concave heat melting cast-iron wagon tongues,
    Dekalb 2-40 stalks blighted like an albino pygmy,
    a five-month-old crawling across a pink J.C. Penney blanket,
    two Evinrude pleasure boats cruising up and down our road.

i remember
    love tugging with sloth in my fur-lined breast,
    an arthritic hand clenched in VFW rage,
    a field of bull thistles ensnared by the Captain America complex,
    two Cambodian whores copulating on a red-white-and-blue blanket.

i remember
    caroling at the county home on a drizzly Christmas Eve,
    crackling latex flesh, eyes turned toward some brave new fantasy,
    four aluminum evergreens, a revolving Edison disk of color,
    nephew's untuned guitar resonating a full octave low.

i remember

    calling "Sandy! Sandy!" in the wee hours of the dawn

    when trolls and fauns take up mental form,

    walking through sniper-infested Saigon streets,

    climbing beanstalks, coconut palms, fog-enshrouded towers.

i remember

    Parsifal engaged in combat with the denizens of evil,

    a puff of ardor cooled by the damp light of reason,

    five drops of cyanide heading down Beelzebub's gullet,

    Karl Marx's shredded eyeballs in Peking's Mao Tse-tung Square.

Old Glory

Should I observe Old Glory riding brashly past,
I'd poke out her cookie-cutter stars,
raze her wedding-cake stripes.

The Annual New Year's Party

I kiss so long
and wish a bounteous new year,
the trimmings on the tree
flap as you close the door.

I've swallowed enough punch
to sink a destroyer,
when the conversation lagged
I went out for a refill.

My present seemed a fiasco
from the way you gushed so loud,
all wonder how this ignoramus
could slip past the censor-gate.

Tiffany has a new boyfriend,
the German department just challenged
classics to a duel,
some dean can't find the bathroom sink.

A stupid joke makes me want to yawn,
I wink at a good-looker three chairs down,
but the cocktails are too strong
and my behavior abominable.

The hostess good-naturedly
packs me off,
like a favorite sloop,
maybe next year I'll be recalled.

Remembering Names

I have trouble remembering names—
Latin and Greek concoctions
of metaphysics long since disproved,
surnames and humorous alliteration,
flattering repetition from sacred books,
the essence tempera-ed over
by accidental chiaroscuro.

Hans and Marguerite in African/Asian eyes?
"featureless" Oriental faces that have no mnemonic hook,
foreign novels and dramas drive me to desperation
because I can't keep the plot or the characters straight,
a voice on the phone identifies his initials,
I strive mightily to fill in the blanks,
George the first . . . George the second . . . George the third.

Individuals blur into pseudonyms,
family villas, and cleverest of all,
artists who belong to anonymous schools,
middle initials are borrowed from grandpa,
transliterations—bowdlerized, mispronounced—
while names are repetitious, indistinct,
familiar faces I can never forget.

But the magic of identification is broken
when I stick some misbegotten label
on a familiar torso—
what difference how the birth certificate reads?

I know a thing—
but not by its precise, analytical, scientific,
arbitrary Linnaeus.

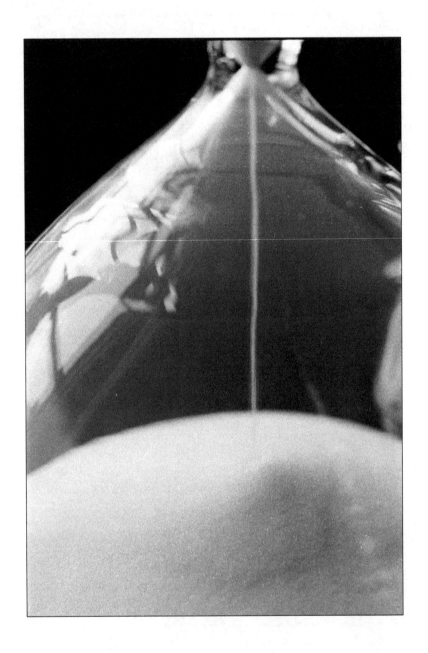

A Class Reunion

Let's not stand on ceremony
after these many years:
how goes it at the mill?
what's your son studying in school?
is your wife cheerful and pressure-sensitive?
what happened to that flute and banjo?
do you travel much?
keep in touch with high school chums?
still collect antique clocks?

Whom do you hear from at Christmas?
see at family reunions?
did they ever raze the Cherry Mansion?
is John still shooting photographs?
Bill has become a cop, Dick, a dentist,
Marv, a Methodist minister,
who did you say was divorced? whose daughter drowned?
they closed that plant down—how many years ago?

Do young lovers still smooch by the river?
the graduating class paint the principal's tires?
are the Meskwakis as far from the town's mainstream
as when we grew up?
the bank has changed hands
and opened up a new branch in Belle Plaine,
a chain bought and knocked down Dick's Restaurant,
they've widened State Street
and cut down all those gorgeous magnolias.

The Bohunks still make fun of the Kasals?
so many have moved back and taken up their dad's vocation
—something they vowed never to do—
sure, I remember those who died in Vietnam,
Doug's in Zimbabwe? John's in Paris?
I can't believe an honors student works in the dime store,
do your ulcers still act up? your arthritis any better?
only 12% of the class graduated from college?

Tom lost his dad's farm,
Loren owns a casino—I
always thought that gambling was a joke—
happy? oh, I get along,
just as unsure as when I was a kid,
you plug yourself in short-term
—jobs, homes, wives—
if you have talent, there's always
some position which pays a livable wage.
        Sure, I still see her,
but she married that fella from out of town.

From My Office in the Flatiron

I thought of you twice already this morning
and it's not even noon,
your happy, happy kisses,
your tender, shy hands.

There's been a ruckus among the secretaries,
and the boss granted one worker leave,
I can't concentrate on this book jacket
or add up five figures in a row.

Three stories down a policeman is handing out a traffic violation,
a blind musician is plucking on his zither,
the "Queen Elizabeth" is docking at pier 41,
and I can almost hear the Statue of Liberty bell.

There's a parade heading up Fifth Avenue,
smiley-faced streamers float past my window,
now it's starting to rain,
my ink smears.

Remorse is as relentless
as the wind-driven pellets:
why didn't I say, "I'm sorry"?
would you have stayed?

False Starts

So many false starts,
haphazard directions and leads,
so many decisions—reversed,
media tried and abandoned,
erasures and blotted-out lines,
so many echoing labyrinths
bringing us face-to-face
with obverse reflections and mirrors.
First a journalist, then a missionary,
now a photographer, a poet next,
Saturn's children are blessed with the urge
but no fortuitous outlet,
like an adolescent whose body confuses.

Once I charted stars hung out
by relatives, later I espied
the nearest and brightest my teachers depicted,
at last I broke off my voyage,
dawdled in eddies and pools.
Breakthrough! Who can stop me now?
I'm soaring weightless and free
on agitated self-generating steam,
elementary motions (it's true)
are awkward-to-impossible,
but the exceptional
is effortless, routine.

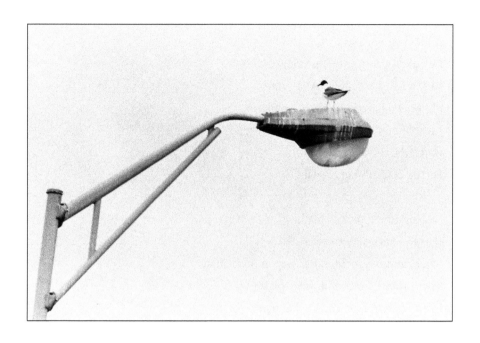

The Laughing Gull

If I had wings like a gull,
I would fly above the turbulent clouds,
so Daedalus escaped his labyrinth,
Phileas Fogg in Jules Verne's balloon,
I would perch on some gregarious spit,
watch the tides reverse,   \
Fortune's tumbling crowns.

I would preen my tail feathers,
soar to regions now concealed,
where temperamental, flip-flop, moody man
hadn't taken a bite and then spit it out,
like a voracious, excreting Pantagruel
or a lecherous, festering Encolpius.

I would travel like Gulliver
to Lucian-satirical, inverted worlds,
poke fun at myself and others caught
in my tickle-ouch net,
inclined by my upbringing
to tall Western tales, while keeping a sober face,
winking with knee-slapping gibes.

I would be as Krishna among the *gopis*,
the prankster Coyote or Spider,
maintain a tease/chuckling relationship
with my wife's sisters' daughters,
calling out to all wayfarers with hairpin, booby trap riddles,

tarring and feathering those dour-faced mammals

until they fly mock-heroic as me

—the laughing Byronic gull of Narragonia.

To Any Future Biographer

I stand corrected,
or at least cast in sufficient doubt,
to warrant rapid backpedaling,
recanting of previously accepted dogmas,
no more cloaking egregious missteps.

I've lived on sheltered suppositions,
followed rote, learned adages,
hedged my bets on more safe numbers than the house,
inched forward at a millipede's pace,
not sufficiently open to fresh gusts of the Spirit,
unable to see beyond my own snorkel and mask.

I haven't felt confident enough about tomorrow
to let my tubers sink down deep,
closed systems make me cringe,
I stare livid at the weakest hypothetical link,
believe the whole world tipsy, brimming toward catastrophe.

Some pan-talents push forward on umpteen different planes,
my scope is limited to one or two acute angles at most,
no doubt you'll label me a hypocrite for a series of perceived U-turns
as I had no crystal ball to avoid shortcomings,
ironic history loves to set
zealous defenders on the wrong side of the wall.

Overall, I've banged together loud, clanging notes and dared to
    call it music,
you, who have an impeccable, sensitive tympanum
will, of course, find it grossly discordant.

My Kitchen Reading Table

What good do these books do me
underlined and frayed?
my head is far too small
to house even a fraction of the world's discoveries.

I'm not a Marco Polo
nor a Richard of the Lion,
my will—stubborn and shortsighted—
scorns advice from "lesser" men.

I peer through iron spectacles,
I plough a plumbline furrow—
where is the deity that I should worship
with sacrifice and oblation?

Like a Kabuki player masked
in the floating, transient world,
I succumb to lower urges
and forget illustrated McGuffey's of the past.

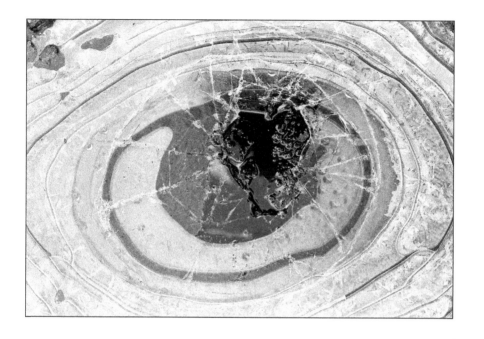

There Was a Boom

There was a boom last night
vibrated me out of bed,
no trumpet or tuba blast,
just a crescendo of revelation.

On the map of my contortions
it bruised the isthmus of hope,
now I limp/lurch perfunctorily,
an id-mangled corpse.

The Realist, or the Cynic

In the Calumny of Apelles, Suspicion wears a crown,
Beauty drags tousled Innocence along,
Justice grows a braying ass's snout.

I myself saw Virtue in the dock,
Intellect flogged, Kindness hanging from a gibbet,
neither Crime nor Deceit reversed.

Ever since that day
my heart palpitates the more,
the sayings of Confucius are like chaff thrown to the wind.

For now I know human nature
and I commit myself to no man's thought.

A Neighbor Died Last Evening

A neighbor died last evening
and, to the best of my knowledge,
I never uttered two distinct syllables
in his direction my entire life,
oh, occasionally we'd tip our hats and wave
as hermits do from their respective holes,
but neither of us had a temperament for cheery banter,
we indignantly thought that the province
of politicians or super-sales-jerks.

What if I had once overcome my customary restraint,
invited in a few I didn't know for a makeshift celebration,
even carved up the fatted calf,
or at least laid out a confectionery surprise;
gregariousness is often forced
except among a band of kindred spirits,
while those with a weak conscience are horrified by any breach
    of protocol.

I had felt smug, complacent,
sure that I would be the first to offer emergency assistance,
but now I've come to realize
no one will ring up a stranger unless other options fade,
friendships must be forged on the anvil and the fire
and require a continual round of stethoscopes and how'd you do's,
while vague, unfamiliar faces—mere acquaintances—
waft in and out like umbrella spores in a haphazard breeze.

After Reading Kenneth Rexroth

No matter what road I take
I'm homeward bound,
    migrating birds flock to the same tree,
    salmon spawn in calm, familiar pools,
    orange monarchs return from a thousand-mile journey,
the welcome mat invites one and all.

Murmurs and coos and yes, it's so's,
the years dissolve after a round or two of chatter,
    I worship at the shrine of "You,"
    old faces, old haunts, old memories,
    while circumstances change,
there's an anchor cutting across generations.

Beneath the still surface: violent tremors,
sunken caverns, life-threatening shapes,
    with incorrect pressure
    Old Faithful will blow.
    Apologies, I'm sorry, excuse my thoughtlessness,
then the waters smooth over.

If I Could Play a Scalar Instrument

If I could play a scalar instrument,
say a guitar or harmonica,
maintain a lilting, dulcet tone,
this might amplify gaiety among friends,
but as it is, I gesticulate wildly, wag my feverish tongue,
heap burgers and dogs onto hospitable flames,
pull out a Doubleday ball and glove, a pinochle deck,
since I don't have access to insider revelations,
nor do I espouse soapbox solutions to the world's indignities,
indeed, mesmerizing multitudes is not my peculiar charism.

What I do is listen and wait, ask penetrating questions,
try to talk more of substance than trifles,
seek out frequencies, resonances worthy of admiration,
then nurture all via calls, letters, stopover visits
amid a madcap carnival of weddings, babies, geographical dislocations,
philosophies which veer to the fore and aft,
I don't want a Hallelujah chorus of synchronized yes-men,
nor a coven of kindred spirits, just sympathetic, blunt truth-tellers
to whom I can throw out an occasional brickbat,
then receive the boomerang back with grace and equanimity.

The Broken Circle

Where have they all gone
who conversed with me so recent ago?
their exuberant, silly banter
lightened a morose, moribund day,
their secure, comforting cadence
drew me beyond the isolated, sickly self,
their strident words of correction
first jostled, then goaded my enlightened reason.

I'll never forget them as long as the "I" continues,
and should the soul burst from its stunted cocoon,
attain the stillness of absorptive contemplation,
I'll hallow their remembrance in rows of votive candles,
rumba before these pinpoints of light,
lift up my hands in Sulpician prayer
for all who beckoned me to the true, unswerving path.

We had such sweet seasons together,
swapped off-white jokes, exchanged a common meal,
offered insulting presents—compared to each other's worth,
attended plays, concerts, art exhibits,
as Triune fellows surrender to jollity,
if one grew too vehement, peace was restored,
ever wary of the boundary between interdependence and suffocation.

If this be love, and I believe it so,
why cling the moldy ivy and moss
to these sobbing slabs of talus?

cemeteries should be star sapphires
where lithe children learn unhurtful games,
in these plots where chrysanthemums wither,
the departed wave and motion us
to weld our severed links and rejoin the broken circle.

When First We Met

Come, sit with me, my love,
and let us recall
how we first stuttered, sent out feelers,
picnicked together on that glorious day,
you considered me inept, a bungler,
I thought you incurably shy—
till we kissed behind the sapling curtain.

What was it we saw in each other:
a tincture of empathy? a modicum of sincerity?
the echo of some faint Hollywood ideal?
the co-mingling of congenial minds?
our first genuinely reciprocated affection?
(did we love or rather love to be loved?)
our eyes glowed like luminous orbs
amid a bright firmament of passions.

Then you blinked or was it I?
the nightmares commenced like surf-pounding waves,
we consumed and were being consumed
by prickly temperaments and hereditary values,
our lives bobbed up and down like unbalanced barometers,
we agreed to disagree,
stagnating into this limbo of intermittent harmony,
a swirling amalgam of disjointed intimacies.

Awake, Sweet William!

Awake, Sweet William!
crab apple and magnolia are already in bloom.
Lift up your head, daisy!
crocus and tulip have yawned and made love.
Still bleary-eyed, my pink-laced beauty,
when nature herself is primped for a banquet or ball?
Then sleep, while you can,
I'm off to join the United Society of Waking Believers
in Jesus' second (more festive) appearing.

Envy

I'm waiting for a monogrammed invitation
to exhibit to everyone I know that I've been chosen
for the highest seat in the inner ring—
yet how does one cozy up to a reluctant host
except by winks and flattery?
still, if the overdue pony express doesn't appear soon,
I'm going to cry.

Or, second option,
perhaps I can prime the rumor mills
with slanted, misleading innuendo
that this piddling party is closed
to all but those who are swollen-headed and their kowtowing lackeys,
and anyone who so much as hints that I'd accept
should be tarred and feathered or hung in effigy.

The Ladder

Life goes on like a faithful ladder,
I move sprightly up the wooden steps,
the air grows thinner
as I leave my native soil.

The exercise is exhilarating
as I stretch forward rung by rung,
though the top is still invisible,
I'm not anxious or afraid.

While some children pell-mell scramble,
others puff and wheeze and dangle,
the pace is not so critical,
just don't always look back.

The key to climbing ladders I've discerned
is both grip and momentum,
loosen either:
the rungs soon start slanting down.

The Introspective Candle

Upon this wick my flame tapers down,
the dripping hot disfigures my smooth young column,
the sevenfold candelabra is like tongues of diverse kind,
> who am I?
> and what spark set me ablaze?
> how can my hot drip wet?
> my oxygen burn in a nitrogen atmosphere?
> whence comes my endless oil?

Some see me as yellow mystery, others defer to Lavoisier's laws,
I turn about and stare at my silver-mercury spectacle,
watch inverted Kepler rods and cones: beneath my flaming circumference,
> is my center cold?
> what have others said?
> and how will my home town vote?
> am I a sickly cutting
> or the choice of my mother's litter?

As tears run down and freeze my flickering joys,
I grow pudgy, sedate, less called-upon,
my skin creased, calloused: am I less self-aware?

The Faithful But Haughty Mirror

The faithful but haughty mirror
is as unforgiving as a Gibbon or a Thucydides,
if I turn round in anger, I catch myself aflame
or if I stare out rose-tinted I decorate myself a hero,
I'm changeable as a chameleon
whose exterior on occasion may please a near-sighted debutante,
but whose interior consists of mildewed, rotting timbers;
we are so obsessed with optic interviews, auto-depictions,
yet who can detect Dorian Gray's heinous crimes from his features?

Still we gaze, scribble out annotations:
how common, how comely, how jubilant, how morose;
like nurses who loiter with one hand in their rectums
inquiring over and over how proximate am I to normal?
is my temperature ascending or descending?
like a professional pollster we long for a stable nay or aye,
which represents, at best, a freeze-action, disintegrating opinion,
as Narcissus proved, mirrors are notoriously wobbly
and those prone to hydromancy may drown.

Reflections are meant to be both silvery and unflattering
as the unsolicited admonitions of a trustworthy friend.

A Hard Night's Labor

I awoke
from a hard night's labor,
the sheet perspiring,
my head spinning in ovals
like a nonstop merry-go-round.

All night long the screech owls,
flying bats, underground denizens,
stealthy predators, kept gnawing
at my dismembered heart,
tearing at the muscular walls.

Like an amnesiac jolted by memory,
I was shaken by incoherent thoughts,
clutched at the wisps of fractured dreams,
images both solemn and redolent,
I had intercourse with the vile dead.

Call the Cumaean Sibyl and her oak leaves
that I might beseech
my discomfited father for advice,
for my grandiose plans have been aborted,
my fence-sitting days are at end.

The Broken Vase

This morning I broke the vase
that my grandmother had given us from her trip to Tainan,
it depicted a weathered sage with a freckled birthmark
plodding through gnarled mountains
carrying a knapsack of rice, a copy of Lao-tzu;
it seemed a pity that a tattered man
should wander thus through this frigid landscape,
but perhaps he'd construct a wood hut, plant two or three
bean sprouts, scratch for herbs with his walking stick;
in the spring cranes might fly overhead,
then he would gather bouquets of sorrel and looking glass,
listen for resounding echoes in the neighboring peaks,
yes, he could make do with so very little.

At first I was sorry
to see his haggard features far from the imperial court
with no retinue of children,
no wife to fuss over his disheveled appearance;
then I thought I heard him sighing, moaning,
but I realized the porcelain surface
acted like a bronze mirror
to hurl back my own hidden, reclusive longings,
maybe the fellow was whistling a carefree tune,
still, I believed it strange he was so misshapen
—was that a tear falling down his left cheek?
then I thought I heard him laughing, singing
in the mountains like mad Po Chü-i.

The Shy and the Vulnerable

I feel awkward in my shy, fluttering ineptness,
like an albatross whose wing-to-body ratio is absurd,
I'm golem, half-formed,
like an adolescent who projects his shadow.

I feel endangered as a passenger pigeon
or that living fossil, the lungfish,
helpless as an invalid borne on a litter,
since I lack the most rudimentary survival skills,
I've become overly reliant on the effusive benevolence of friends.

So rather than lingering before full-length mirrors—
I'm appalled at Rembrandt's unretouched self-portraits:
those harsh, brutal truth-tellers—
I don costumes like any quick-change artist who seeks to amuse
    his companions,
aware that my vaunted independence is a tissue of lies.

I inch forward, crawl,
camouflaging my face with pinions,
lest I appear to weep or to blush in full view,
for my soul is sealed, or I should say, entombed,
in an inviolate, shatter-proof, impenetrable vault.

Self-Siege

I have declared battle against myself,
set up siegeworks, employed flamethrowers,
released armor-piercing arrows
against my most flagrant towers,
been traitor-breached to the innermost keep.

I've a Tenuous Hold

I've a tenuous hold on the world
a Jericho trumpet could sunder
with one crescendo.
Unwinding my spool of psychogenesis,
magic arias I hear,
friends tower like Samson Agonistes.

The *Weltschmerz* I traverse
in Kafka's sheltering chariot,
its boundaries, thin and fluid,
can be punctured by a song;
I feel hungry, am athirst
for the marvelous-fantastic.

Oh, that I were a Cyprinid
swimming in a school of self-repeating
molecules; instead I row up and down
my shelves, one Hilarious Bookbinder,
Pseudodoxia Epidemica,
my brushstrokes—indelible as ochre.

I strike with the "poisoned hand,"
I pounce with the "scorpion sting."
In burnt sienna, lampblack, Venetian red,
I sigh, yet suffer from *camera obscura*.

The Way of Heaven is inlaid Hepplewhite feather;
however, folkshooter that I am,

I drive nails with scrap-iron bullets,
release my turtle-claw arrows,
down a couple of Pink Ladies, flip open
my frog-mouth visor—to run.

"In Pisa, they say, he received the stigmata,
visible on request, only to himself."
(P.S. More likely it was a self-inflicted wound
just before he was declared AWOL.)

The Duke of Anarchy

I am the Duke of Anarchy,
the Earl of Discord,
Prince of the Nut House Gang.

Down

Down the abysmal shafts of abandoned coal mines,
past the stinking flesh of the black hole of Calcutta,
Through the murky graves of Mariana Trench,
where even the light of heaven is extinguished,
Down the geothermal cavities
which the spelunker dares not explore,
hotter than the infernal regions where His Majesty reigns,
Down to the core of our being which issues into eternal life.

Here every decision of consequence
is eagerness betrayed by immobility:
will I serve my essence or yet another accident,
will my particular be absorbed in your universal?
Or shall I Walden-like swim to the surface
through waters permeated by my own insincerity
and break through the gravity of my own ambition?

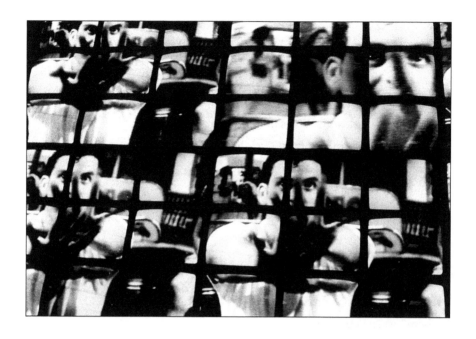

Guilt

Avenues awash with self-indulgence,
backroads bogged down with "it might have been,"
eddies filling up with half-hearted promises,
ice breakers stuck at the bergs of indifference,
feeble monads shrinking from the light
in this second best of all possible worlds,
divine stethoscope listening for compassion—
embarrassed to hear fail-safe excuses.

Blessings upon you Man of Sorrows
for pricking the balloons of my self-confidence,
requiring a slapstick retreat from too many countenances
where I ween your visage,
frankly, I find religion a detriment to piety,
a veneer of good intentions
papering over guilt and heartache,
Norman Vincent Peale superficiality—
good manners mistaken for morality.

Right and wrong catalogued in Aquinas' *Summa*,
the Talmud of Christendom,
unable to cope with open invitations to love,
existential quandaries
you can't look up in the rule books,
spiritual exercises familiar
to only the greatest of saints,
vices and virtues an electron microscope can't segregate.

Cleavage between thought and deed,
cavernous assumptions shaken by tremors of fear,
leopards changing their spots
—can't tell which is real—
sinking into the quicksand of abstract irrelevance
or the dark night of self-inflicted wounds,
scattered images beyond the looking glass,
3-D luminescent puzzles.

This is the way religion pains—
with museums of relics you can touch,
but which don't work miracles today.

Secular City

We break solidarity with our fellows
when we say, "I'm saved,"
get up of a Sunday morning
and glory in the Word come down from God.

Perhaps their faith doesn't need a lift
in the incensed surroundings of worshipping believers,
nor do they require a musical interlude
in the deadening monotone of unharmonic existence,
maybe they can celebrate with the pantheists
a natural, Wordsworthian splendor.

I don't blame those
who won't be stuffed into coat or tie
—nor will I—
how can God possibly take offense
if our lips are pursed in sincere prayer?
the one sacrifice he elicits
is a slashed and bleeding heart.

Maybe some object to bigots, "archaic" strictures on sex,
noblesse oblige conservatism,
frontlets daubed in acrimony;
well, I didn't come to the temple
to bind my hands,
but to break loose from stifling convention.

Here's where I part
with those Sabbath-malingerers,
because I want to be transcended,
feel culpable, go home brooding
over personal and professional relations,
maybe even stop in the hurly-burly of my own ambition
and be deflected.

God's bigger than our religious teachers ever imagined;
don't be queasy,
he hasn't moved;
he's just as accessible and companionable
as when you were a child.

I Confess to . . .

an inordinate disgust for ostentation,
relatively minor self-sacrifice,
words more beautiful than deeds.

short-fused thunder,
envy, spite, and jealousy,
tainted motives.

a tongue for connotation,
Faustian lusts,
a social mask that mutters, "How interesting."

an undeniable self-righteousness,
exaggeration when provoked,
oh, too many witticisms.

spouting controversial
when I'm somewhere near the mean,
scrutinizing tolerance granted
in the name of "no conviction."

a guilt that handicaps my race,
being overly observant of protocol,
openness nearing hubris,
a hang-up about repeating.

superficially sensitive ears and eyes,
weeping far too frequently,
purifying the inner man,
letting my neighbor go.

Psalm 42

I said to my soul,
"Arise and be not cast down!"
lingering nigh unto despair,

tumbling past cataracts
and flumes, comingling
in a tear duct salty sea.

"Why so punctured, slashed,
limp, worn thin,
battered by the waves?

O my soul, darkened with
poor counsel, weighed down by
cynicism and by fears ballooned:

Keep vigilant and staid!"
With your armor of self-reliance,
a lance to upend the netherworld,

you rout foes (imaginary),
levitate in mid-air.
At the Temple of Dethroned Idols

you blow bubbles of glass,
like a Philistine or Hittite
you strut about and then you fall.

In the denouement
from which prompter will you take your cue?
and who'll pray for your ascent?

I Present My Heart:

then I receive it back as from a jeweler,
who has aligned the erring ruby
and oiled the sticking cam,
set the pendulum in tuning fork motion,
caesium resolute as a Greenwich mean;
yes, perhaps now some will stop, check,
even synchronize their movements
by heaven's more precise arterial time.

Not I, But Christ

I, moist, feeble light,
Christ, a blow furnace of concern,
mine, the cool, rational flame,
his, the red-hot activist torch,
me, the sputtering wick, him, the Roman candle.
It's me on the cross,
he's an onlooker now.
It's me who'll die,
he's on death's other shore.

First, he discerns the temptation
I'm called to avoid;
my flesh pulls like a witching rod,
so that I conquer death, sin and pain
with his indwelling power.
I'm the skeleton in which he pours his love,
I reciprocate more like Pavlov's dog.

He's free, I'm in fetters,
I'm gutted, he's ebullient.
He came down that I might be seated on high,
I repose in my casket till he upsets my cadaver.
Not he, but I, will ascend at Gabriel's signal;
he, not I, has initiated a full millennium of celebration.

I, the creature,

he's the firstborn in pre-eminence,

he, the drill sergeant, I, his private first-class,

he, my Zeus, I, his Mercury,

I knock, he escorts,

he beckons, I fall in place.

I adore, he dazzles,

he ravishes, I, an orgasm;

once we were two and unequal,

now mystic married, we love in cohesion.

I, his Plato, he, my Socrates,

he, my star, I, his revolving planet,

me, the sublunar, him, the primum mobile,

me, the vessel, him, the intoxicating beverage,

me, simulacrum, him, uncreated stratum,

him, the bestower, me the dawdling recipient,

he inspires, while I just scrounge about for syllables,

he's the exemplum, I, more often the contrarian.

I Stand by the Door

I stand by the door
and invite passers-by
to enter in and be saved.

From the ceiling hang healing lanterns,
inside a preacher stands rigid, yet compassionate,
before him in guilty, uncomfortable pews,
a fellowship intercedes/adores,
partaking of those twin rituals of cleansing and discernment.

One who desires harmony, unity, and enlightenment
had better create a self-mirroring church,
for here Christ's body bleeds and hurts,
is sacrificed in a hundred daily agonies,
collectively advances, then retreats.

Circus barkers beckon audiences to spectacle,
3-ring entertainment, masquerade,
keepers of the door, on the other hand, commend discipleship,
effacement, even joyful abandon, o taste and see
the broken-absent one, sacramentally present within our midst.

Flim-flam artists and con men
prove loud, importuning buttonholers,
offer animated, see-you-at-the-top schemes,
our message, however, is of a different sort, simple though obscure,
behold the lion-lamb, heed his fiery injunctions and live.

I Said . . .

I said to these stones,
"Give me your strength, your endurance,
that I may be just as unperturbed
by the eddies and currents of time."

I said to the staunch, upright trees,
"Make me a bulwark
against blustery, prevailing elements,
so spindly plants can shelter near my base."

I said to the rivers
cross-winding relentlessly toward shore,
"May I carry such a heavy, sluggish
load with equal grace and poise."

I said to the clouds,
"Raise me above lead mortals
to white heights of scudding significance,
light-hearted as a balloon."

I said to the moon, so shimmering and true,
"Hand me a face of bold radiance,
so any frightened by pitch-black darkness
can look here to steady their trembling brows."

I said to the feathery, lighter-than-air creatures,
"Would that I could float with such effortless ease,

dancingly land and take off,
intone such melodious scales."

I said to the fluttering fish,
streamlined, sleek, and cold,
"If only I could be so taciturn, yet wise,
content to swim within my prescribed domain."

I said to the alluvial soil—
pulverized by glaciers, ground into tillable clumps—
"How wonderful if I were more pliable, productive,
the longer I'm tossed about."

I said to the air
—fresh, carefree, and strong—
"Let me, too, be unobtrusive, invisible
in all of the works I carry out."

A Rainbow—Slain

I met a rainbow on the road and slew it,
dismembered its colored prisms,
gave the yellowish chunks to my wife,
the red and green bands to my children.

My skin blazed up as in a halo,
having rubbed up against that splendiferous palette,
no solvent could wash Cain's glimmering fingers,
it was the arc that set me off.

I'm absolutely disgusted by ellipses, parabolas,
any figures formed by the twin pointers of a compass,
I'm livid, too, at finding an empty bucket on my stray end,
while some usurper counts gold doubloons on the other.

Bright things come out only after the rain,
yet this flimsy gauze is insubstantial, evanescent
—unlike our corporeal forms—
for the colors bleed, aren't crisply defined.

How good that I removed that ugly hunchback
serpent from the ethereal heavens
before it could generate faint, secondary offspring, colors reversed—
has anyone before performed a rainbow vasectomy?

The world is better off in dreary monochrome,
false hopes can't be lifted up and squashed,

harmonies are fully realized only in pure achromatic scales, otherwise, we end up forever chasing crayon sundogs.

Flipping Ripe Avocados

Backpedaling on my unicycle
I flip ripe avocados
in a sing-song sleight-of-hand,
anxious to see which will be the first
to make a luminous splat.

Pointy-hatted clowns squeeze out mascara from tubes,
crooners belt out lovelorn ditties,
actors rat-a-tat-tat pantomime
till weariness intervenes
in a revolving, stroboscopic, stop-action routine.

Crowds roar with huzzahs, toss high their caramel corn,
though I've no high-wire act or tiger of my own,
just phosphorescent flares and simulated bowling pins,
I can sip liquids from a disappearing cup
amid these high-flying pinwheel whirlers.

I'm more like a sideshow to a sideshow,
an outer ring to the main attraction,
could never win crowd-o-meter ratings,
nor take top billing in a Ringling Brothers/Barnum & Bailey poster,
but neither, however, am I likely to break open my hypothalamus.

Two-Stepping with Snowflakes

Imagined:
I'm two-stepping with snowflakes
in a hexagonal tête-à-tête,
curtsying on tiptoe,
allemande left, Virginia reel right,
till I flip cartwheels in mid-air.

I'm throwing out my hip,
dislocating my little finger,
drum-pounding with elbows and joints,
while other partners minuet in clogs,
I hokey-cokey, promenade,
pirouette, click heels, evaporate.

Actual:
By putting one awkward foot before its neighbor,
I twist on spindly ankles,
leap high on cement balls and arches;
beside these debonair, freefall artists,
who resemble glass ballerina spinnerettes,
I appear a waltzing brontosaurus.

Chief Keeper of the Parrots

I would be Chief Keeper of the Parrots
under Suleiman the Magnificent,
teach each bird to recite the 99 names of Allah
(or the 101 titles Our Emperor claims),
they'll sing of Sinan, his domed splendor and pencil minarets,
Barbarossa, unconquerable on the Mediterranean,
the latest fortress captured by our siege-work Janissaries,
overhear the whisperings of Roxelana near the fountain of intrigue
or the stratagems of our grand vizier, Ibrahim Pasha,
while admiring glittering saz scrolls,
brocaded silk and velvet balls.

Praise be to Allah
for the wisdom given to our illustrious administrator/sage,
promoting talent from far-flung provinces,
patron to gold and silver engravers,
guarantor of freedom to all three peoples of the book,
why, he's the foremost lawgiver to arise from the house of Osman.
Still, my favorite haunt will be
the polyglot bazaar where hawkers sell their choicest seeds,
veiled women stroll, haggling over pomegranates or halal lambs,
Egyptian shadow puppets perform episodes from *One Thousand and
One Nights*,
couriers speed by, conveying tribute from another subdued realm,
while Suleiman the Gracious allows for a disgruntled remark
to pass with no obvious repercussions.

119

Another World

Last night I lusted after another world—
tetrahedral crystal,
black-banded onyx
—dash your head against Gibraltar:

Solid, serene, impervious to Poseidon,
frieze, girder, Corinthian column.
Fluctuation's banned,
Inconsistency's punished
in architectonic Xanadu.

Here we sing syllogistic nursery rhymes,
calculate utilitarian succor,
admire King Djoser's tomb,
worship *l'homme machine.*

Heraclitus swallowed up by Parmenides,
Newton browbeating Heisenberg,
Aquinas cremating Schleiermacher.

Peaceable kingdom
ohne electricity
—flat, not undulating—
Laplace's predictable atoms
sympathetic as a data processor.

Digital flowers, golden symmetry,
proportional meals like a diabetic's,
counterpoint John Philip Sousa,
Prussian regimen, internal tick-tock.

Emotion's too sporadic,
love's uncontrollable,
excessive energy must be jettisoned
through the gates of horn.

Anatomy scan every hour,
replaceable arms, ligaments, and motors—
magnetic brains,
gyroscopic order.

Push the buttons:
RECORD   START
STOP   REWIND
no manual override.

Society's automatically oiled,
or more likely opiated,
every bolt has its nut,
every foot, a custom-made moccasin.

No rough edges,
no solder or glue,
peak efficiency, optimum adjustment—
a technician's utopia.

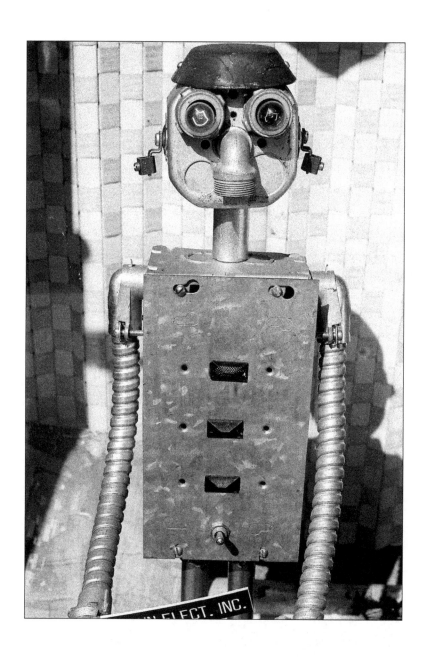

Technical Profundities

I've heard the serenade of an advancing dune,
watched rainbows split apart into falling prisms,
crossbred mice—mottled and striped—
been burned by water from a geothermal mist,
observed ice-covered trees shake off their transparent manacles,
balls of lightning, electro-magnetic storms, black, vacuumous spouts,
witnessed tinctures of iodine turn aqua and smoky,
microwave meat appear pink from "the inside out,"
listened to dead celebrities croon on a flat plastic disk,
grown a single crystal whisker mightier than the entire "beard,"
these are profundities too much for my untechnical mind.

Out of Favor

I'm not in the loop any more
as one who basks in the emperor's favor,
mandarins have crept in and seized the channels of power,
belittled my paltry presence,
now messages are passed on—garbled—
via puffed-up intermediaries,
my light is fading fast
and I had but few premonitions why,
did some stray utterance lead to an imagined slight?
is my gruff, plain-spoken manner
ill-suited to this clandestine, backstabbing crowd?
has a spy infiltrated our inner circle, revealed my profoundest doubts?

Why am I so distraught, since each elevation
contains the double helix of its own demise?
of late I've come to be regarded as a crotchety magpie
whose cawings have been the brunt of winks and gibes,
this new generation of confidants has stifled all honest dissent,
but perhaps I should be comforted
that I'm *not* held up for corporate ridicule, labeled an incendiary,
or hunted down by designated assassins,
I can still retire to some secluded refuge,
discreetly scribble out my memoirs, rebut bloated sycophants,
so for now the sanest policy would be to swallow my inordinate pride,
as history is heaped up with cartloads of corpses
who gave wiser, sounder counsel than my own.

In the Winter of My Prime

Thou seest me in the winter of my prime,
when icy love cracks and bends
under too passionate an embrace,
when semen swim sluggish
up their appointed tubes,
grow double tails, deformed heads,
their ardor too cool to penetrate an egg,
when my sap is shrunk—devoid of chlorophyll—
 my limbs outstretched, bare, like a flat, twisted scarecrow,
a whimpering skeleton of former days.

In Old Age

Not much remains:
    a winsome wrinkle,
        a self-confident strut,
            a shock of gray.

My thoughts all run into familiar grooves
or I revert to facile childhood fantasies,
the world recedes into ribbons and bows
or nightmares stark out of Ingmar Bergman.

I hurt, but to whom shall I speak?
    my friends are all interred,
        my son and daughter estranged,
        this rosé no longer lightens my step.

      I amble about in spurts,
I shuffle in slippers,
            what is an elderberry
          compared to days gone by?

In my mind's eye the—expletive deleted—
abacus keeps adding up,
        my frayed sleeves and sagging crotch,
        a yawning wife nearby.

Little things bother me more:
    haughty clerks, slow checks, bad service,

satires on death,
the minister reads of heaven from his seminary books.

And I can't whistle to God,
my logic bins are empty,
          as if life itself leaked in,
I'm shaky, unsure,
like a child gazing at a grasshopper
or the moon.

          I sip slowly my coffee,
          savor my morning toast,
          henceforth clocks will be my enemy,
          Methuselah, how could you endure so long?

Last night I vomited,
now my bowels moved,
          I have enough fight left for a skirmish
          but not a siege,
et omnia vanitas.

                    Globe-trottingly hoarse—
     contentment eludes us the farther downstream,
would that the witch of Endor prophesied a more noble fate,
          I'm woozy . . . are the chairs that far
                              overhead?

Listing of Photographs

Works Cited

Abrams, M.H. *The Mirror and the Lamp: Romantic Theory and the Critical Tradition.* Oxford University Press: New York, 1971.

Akutagawa, Ryunosuke. *Rashomon and Other Stories.* Translated by Takashi Kojima. Bantam: New York, 1959.

Barzun, Jacques. *From Dawn to Decadence: 1500 to the Present.* HarperCollins: New York, 2001.

Baudelaire, Charles. *Paris Spleen: 1869.* Translated by Louise Varese. New Directions: New York, 1970.

Bernard, Oliver, ed. and trans. *Rimbaud.* Penguin: Baltimore, 1962.

Booth, Wayne C. *The Rhetoric of Fiction.* University of Chicago Press: Chicago, 1970.

Bridgwater, Patrick, ed. and trans. *Twentieth-Century German Verse.* Penguin: Baltimore, 1963.

Browning, Robert. *Poems of Robert Browning,* edited by Donald Smalley. Riverside: Cambridge, MA, 1956.

Burckhardt, Sigurd. *Shakespearean Meanings.* Princeton University Press: Princeton, NJ, 1968.

Byron, George Gordon. *Byron, A Self-Portrait: Letters and Diaries 1798 to 1824,* edited by Peter Quennell. Oxford University Press: New York, 1990.

Cary, Phillip. *Philosophy and Religion in the West, Parts 1–3.* The Teaching Company: Chantilly, VA, 1999.

Cole, Toby and Helen Krich Chinoy, eds. *Actors on Acting: Theories, Techniques and Practices.* Crown: New York, 1949.

Craig, Hardin. *Shakespeare: Revised Edition.* Scott, Foresman and Company: Chicago. 1958.

Dickinson, Emily. *Letters, Volume 2,* edited by Mabel Loomis Todd. Roberts Brothers: Boston, 1894.

Diderot, Denis. *The Paradox of Acting* and William Archer, *Masks or Faces?* Hill and Wang: New York, 1957.

Eliot. T.S. *The Elder Statesman: A Play.* Farrar, Straus and Cudahy: New York, 1959.

———. *On Poetry and Poets.* Noonday: New York, 1961.

———. *Selected Prose of T.S. Eliot,* edited by Frank Kermode. Harcourt/Farrar, Straus, and Giroux: New York, 1980.

Ellmann, Richard. *Yeats: The Man and His Masks.* E.P. Dutton: New York, 1948.

Empson, William. *Seven Types of Ambiguity.* New Directions: New York, 1966.

Garff, Joakim. *Soren Kierkegaard: A Biography.* Translated by Bruce H. Kirmmse. Princeton University Press: Princeton, 2005.

Gide, André. *The Counterfeiters* with *Journal of "The Counterfeiters."* Translated by Dorothy Bussy and Justin O'Brien. Modern Library: New York, 1955.

———. *If It Die: An Autobiography.* Translated by Dorothy Bussy. Modern Library: New York, 1935.

———. *The Journals of André Gide, Volume 1: 1889–1924.* Edited and translated by Justin O'Brien. Vintage: New York, 1961.

————. *The Journals of André Gide: 1914–1927*. Translated by Justin O'Brien. Alfred Knopf: New York, 1947.

Gilbert, Allan H., ed. *Literary Criticism: Plato to Dryden*. Wayne State University Press: Detroit, 1970.

Goethe, Johann Wolfgang. *Faust: Part One and Part Two*. Translated by Charles E. Passage. Bobbs-Merrill: Indianapolis, 1965.

Gudas, Fabian, "Persona." In *The New Princeton Encyclopedia of Poetry and Poetics*, edited by Alex Preminger and T.V.F. Brogan, 901. Princeton University Press: Princeton, 1993.

Guterman, Norbert, compiler. *The Anchor Book of French Quotations with English Translations*. Anchor: New York, 1990.

Halsall, A.W., "*Memoires D'Outre-Tombe.*" In *Encyclopedia of the Romantic Era, 1760–1850, Volume 2*, edited by Christopher John Murray, 725. Fitzroy Dearborn: Chicago, 2004.

Hamburger, Michael. *The Truth of Poetry: Tensions in Modern Poetry from Baudelaire to the 1960s*. Harcourt Brace Jovanovich: New York, 1969.

Hays, H.R., trans. *The Selected Writings of Juan Ramón Jiménez*, edited by Eugenio Florit. Grove: New York, 1957.

Jones, W.R., trans. *A New Dictionary of Quotations from Greek, Latin, and Modern Languages Translated into English*. J.B. Lippincott: Philadelphia, 1869.

Keats, John. *Selected Letters of John Keats*, edited by Robert Pack. New American Library: New York, 1974.

Kierkegaard, Soren. *Works of Love*. Translated by Howard and Edna Hong. Harper & Row: New York, 1980.

Kracauer, Siegried. *Theory of Film: The Redemption of Physical Reality*. Oxford University Press: New York, 1970.

Laforgue, Jules. *Poésies complètes*. Leon Vanier: Paris, 1894.

Lattimore, Richmond, trans. *The Iliad of Homer*. University of Chicago Press: Chicago, 1961.

Lewis, W.S., "The Difficult Art of Biography." In *Biography Past and Present: Selected and Critical Essays*, edited by William H. Davenport and Ben Sigel, 65. Charles Scribner's Sons: New York, 1965.

Lowrie, William. *Kierkegaard, Volume 1*. Harper & Brothers: New York, 1962.

Mandelbaum, Allen and Robert D. Richardson, Jr., eds. *Three Centuries of American Poetry: 1620–1923*. Bantam: New York, 1999.

Montaigne, Michel Eyquem de. *The Complete Essays of Montaigne*. Translated by Donald M. Frame. Stanford University Press: Stanford, CA, 1979.

Mounce, William D. *Mounce's Complete Expository Dictionary of Old and New Testament Words*. Zondervan: Grand Rapids, 2006.

Novalis. *Hymns to the Night and Other Selected Writings*. Translated by Charles E. Passage. Bobbs-Merrill: Indianapolis, 1960.

Paul, Sherman. *The Shores of America: Thoreau's Inward Exploration*. University of Illinois Press: Urbana, IL, 1972.

Pessoa, Fernando. *The Book of Disquiet*, edited and translated by Richard Zenith. Penguin: New York, 2003.

————. *A Little Larger Than the Entire Universe: Selected Poems*, edited and translated by Richard Zenith. Penguin: New York, 2006.

———. *Selected Poems*, edited and translated by Peter Rickard. University of Texas Press: Austin, 1971.

———. *The Selected Prose of Fernando Pessoa*, edited and translated by Richard Zenith. Grove: New York, 2001.

Peyre, Henri. *Literature and Sincerity*. Yale University Press: New Haven, CT, 1969.

Plutarch. *The Rise and Fall of Athens*. Translated by Ian Scott-Kilvert. Penguin: New York, 1976.

Pound, Ezra. *The Cantos of Ezra Pound*. New Directions: New York, 1970.

———. *Ezra Pound: Translations, Enlarged Edition*. New Directions: New York, 1963.

———. *A Memoir of Gaudier-Brzeska*. New Directions: New York, 1960.

———. *New Selected Poems and Translations, Second Edition*, edited by Richard Sieburth. New Directions: New York, 2010.

Pritchard, William H. *Lives of the Modern Poets*. Oxford University Press: New York, 1981.

Rees, William, ed. and trans. *French Poetry: 1820–1950*. Penguin: New York, 1990.

Reid, Alastair, trans., "We Are Many." In *The Vintage Book of Contemporary World Poetry*, edited by J.D. McClatchy, 528. Vintage: New York, 1996.

Ross, W.D., trans. "Metaphysics." In *The Complete Works of Aristotle, Volume 2*, edited by Jonathan Barnes, 1570. Princeton University Press: Princeton, 1991.

Rousseau, Jean-Jacques. *Julie, or The New Heloise*. Translated and annotated by Philip Stewart and Jean Vache. University Press of New England: Hanover, NH, 1997.

Russell, John, trans. *The Correspondence between Paul Claudel and André Gide: 1899–1926*. Beacon: Boston, 1964.

Sage, Robert, ed. and trans. *The Private Diaries of Stendhal*. Doubleday: Garden City, NY, 1954.

Scholes, Robert and Robert Kellogg. *The Nature of Narrative*. Oxford University Press: New York, 1971.

Stern, Philip Van Doren, ed. *The Portable Poe*. Penguin: New York, 1979.

Stork, Charles Wharton, trans. *The Lyrical Poems of Hugo Von Hofmannsthal*. Yale University Press: New Haven, CT, 1918.

Tennyson, Alfred Lord. *The Poetic and Dramatic Works of Alfred Lord Tennyson*. Houghton Mifflin: Boston, 1899.

Tournier, Paul. *The Meaning of Persons*. Translated by Edwin Hudson. SCM: London, 1970.

Trilling, Lionel. *Sincerity and Authenticity*. Harvard University Press: Cambridge, MA, 1972.

Valéry, Paul. *Collected Works of Paul Valéry, Volume 2: Poems in the Rough*. Translated by Hilary Corke. Princeton University Press: Princeton, 2015.

———. *The Art of Poetry*. Translated by Denise Folliot. Vintage: New York, 1961.

Wallenstein, Barry. *Visions and Revisions: An Approach to Poetry*. Thomas Y. Crowell: New York, 1971.

Warnke, Frank J. *European Metaphysical Poetry*. Yale University Press: New Haven, CT, 1974.

West, Jessamyn, "The Slave Cast Out." In *The Living Novel: A Symposium*, edited by Granville Hicks, 202. Collier: New York, 1957.

Wheelock, John Hall, ed. *Editor to Author: The Letters of Maxwell Perkins*. Grosset & Dunlap: New York, 1950.

Woledge, Brian, Geoffrey Brereton and Anthony Hartley, eds. *The Penguin Book of French Verse*. Penguin: New York, 1980.

WORKS CITED

Young, Malcolm Clemens. *The Spiritual Journal of Henry David Thoreau*. Mercer University Press: Macon, GA, 2009.

CPSIA information can be obtained
at www.ICGtesting.com
Printed in the USA
LVHW051208311221
707506LV00002B/7